FOOTPRINTS on the MOON

Alexandra Siy

iai Charlesbridge

It's the brightest object in our night sky. A big yellow-white disk, it shrinks to a silver sliver and disappears. Then it's born again, growing full, bright, and mysterious. Throughout the centuries, the Moon's changing face has beckoned us silently. We have looked and wondered, imagined and dreamed.

Twenty-four astronauts have crossed the vast ocean of space that separates Earth and Moon. Twelve have left footprints.

As the Moon orbits Earth, we see the Moon's phases, or a changing portion of the Moon's sunlit surface visible from Earth. This crescent Moon is waxing, which means from day to day we see more of the Moon's sunlit area.

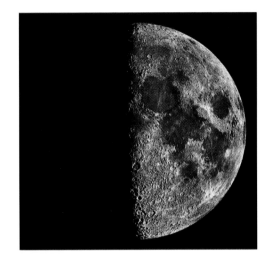

One half of the Moon's sunlit portion is visible in this first-quarter Moon, which has completed one fourth of its orbit.

This crescent Moon is waning, which means the portion of the sunlit surface we see is decreasing. Soon only the farside (the side that always faces away from Earth) will be lit, and the Moon will not be visible from Earth. That phase of the Moon is called a new Moon.

A full Moon occurs when the side of the Moon facing Earth is completely lit by the Sun.

Three quarters of the sunlit portion of the Moon is seen in this waxing gibbous Moon.

bout four thousand years ago, prehistoric people watched the rising and setting Moon at Stonehenge, a temple built from massive stones that were arranged for keeping track of the motions of the Moon, the Sun, and the stars.

Nearly two thousand years later, the ancient Greeks thought that the Moon's dark areas were oceans and the bright spots were land.

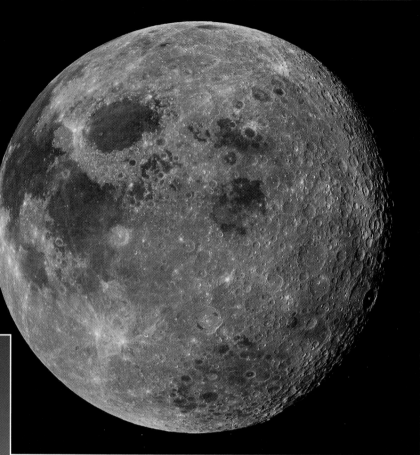

The Moon as photographed by *Apollo 17* astronauts. The bright, rugged highlands are *terrae*, which is Latin for "land." The dark areas are low, flat plains named *maria*, which is Latin for "seas."

Stonehenge, located on Great Britain's Salisbury Plain, at dusk.

This woodcut print of the Moon as seen through a telescope was among the first published by Galileo.

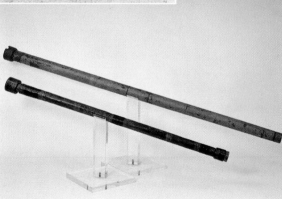

Galileo's telescopes made objects appear nearly one thousand times larger.

In 1610 the Italian scientist and inventor Galileo Galilei published a book called *The Starry Messenger*. The book described the Moon and stars as they appeared in his handmade spyglass, or telescope. Galileo was amazed to see that the Moon's surface was covered with tall mountains and deep craters.

Galileo Galilei (1564-1642) argued that Earth and the other planets circle the Sun. He was imprisoned for the final eight years of his life for contradicting the belief that Earth was the center of the universe.

Although the telescope made the heavens look closer, space travel was still just a dream. That dream suddenly seemed achievable at the dawn of the twentieth century. In 1903, Orville Wright piloted the first airplane, and in 1926 the inventor Robert H. Goddard launched the first liquid-fueled rocket.

Less than twenty years later, powerful rockets were used as weapons in World War II. After the war, scientists worked on rockets for space travel. Daring test pilots, who later became the world's first astronauts, pushed the limits of aviation by flying planes to the outer edge of Earth's atmosphere. Now space was within reach!

Robert H. Goddard stands next to his rocket, which was launched on March 16, 1926. The rocket accelerated upward for 2.5 seconds, reaching a height of 41 feet.

On December 17, 1903, at Kitty Hawk, North Carolina, Orville and Wilbur Wright's plane flew a distance of 120 feet and remained in the air for 12 seconds.

The desire to explore space became an intense competition between the United States and the Soviet Union (modern-day Russia and its former republics). The two countries were enemies in the "cold war," a conflict that threatened the world with nuclear destruction despite the lack of actual combat. One of the fiercest "battles" was the space race.

The Soviets took the lead in 1957 when they launched *Sputnik I*, the world's first artificial satellite. In 1961 a Soviet, Yuri Gagarin, became the first person in space. The American pilot Alan Shepard was the second. On May 25, 1961, President John F. Kennedy declared that before the end of the decade, the United States would try to send a man to the Moon and return him safely to Earth. The space race now had a finish line, and the United States was determined to get there first.

In 1962 President Kennedy examines *Friendship 7*, in which John Glenn (standing behind Kennedy) became the first American to orbit the earth.

In 1958 the National Aeronautics and Space Administration (NASA) was created. NASA's Mercury project was formed to put humans into space. The first Mercury astronauts were (left to right): Walter M. Schirra Jr., Alan B. Shepard Jr., Donald K. Slayton, Virgil I. "Gus" Grissom, John H. Glenn, L. Gordon Cooper Jr., and M. Scott Carpenter.

The crew of *Apollo 1* (left to right): Virgil I. Grissom, Edward H. White II, and Roger B. Chaffee.

Project Gemini (1964-1966) tested new equipment and skills such as rendezvous, the meeting of space vehicles while in Earth's orbit. Project Apollo was next; its mission was to fly men to the Moon.

The race to the Moon demanded the hard work and dedication of at least 400,000 people. The fast pace also took its toll. On January 27, 1967, the crew of *Apollo 1* died in a fire inside the command module during a practice countdown on the launchpad. The next command module was carefully redesigned to correct several fatal flaws, including a cabin door that was almost impossible to open from the inside.

After several unmanned test missions, *Apollo 7* was the first Apollo manned mission and the first U.S. spacecraft to carry three people. Less than two years after the *Apollo 1* tragedy, *Apollo 8* was aimed at the Moon. It was a bold plan: Three astronauts would orbit the Moon and return to Earth.

The *Apollo 7* commander, Wally Schirra, orbited Earth for ten days.

As a *Gemini 4* astronaut, Ed White became the first American to walk in space.

The *Apollo 8* crew trains inside a centrifuge, which simulates the feeling of traveling in space.

The *Apollo 8* astronauts, Commander Frank Borman, James A. Lovell Jr., and William A. Anders, were ready for the adventure. On December 21, 1968, they became the first people to blast off atop the 363-foot-tall Saturn V rocket.

It took sixty-nine hours to reach the Moon. On Christmas Eve, 1968, *Apollo 8* flew around the Moon. For the first time ever, humans saw the lunar farside, a view previously seen only in photographs taken by an unmanned probe. On the farside, radio transmissions to Earth were impossible, and the astronauts lost contact with Mission Control.

On the knee pad of his flight suit, Jim Lovell drew a picture that became the emblem for the first mission to the Moon.

BORMAN LOVELL ANDERS

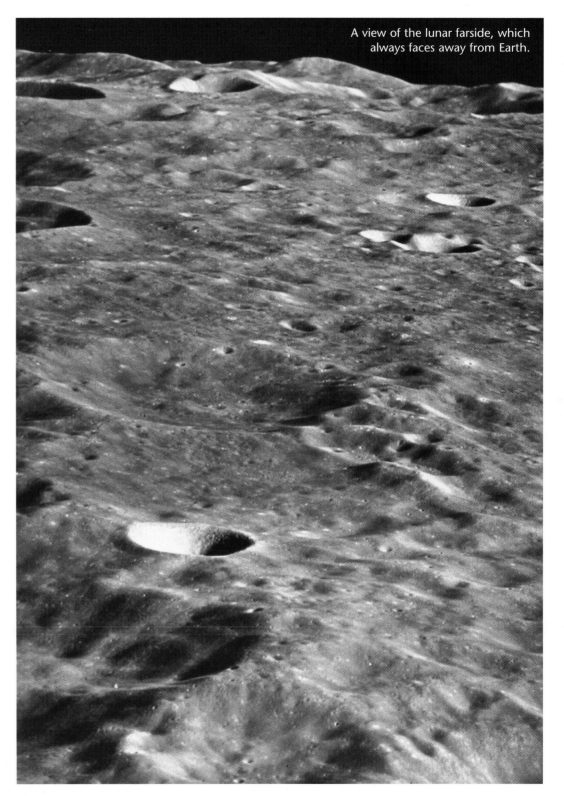

A view of the lunar farside, which always faces away from Earth.

Back above the near side, the unexpected sight of Earth rising above the barren Moon stunned the astronauts.

"Oh, my God! Look at that picture over there," Commander Borman said, taking a black-and-white photograph. Bill Anders quickly loaded a roll of color film into the camera and took two more photographs of earthrise.

"This is *Apollo 8*, coming to you live from the Moon," Commander Borman announced.

The astronauts were broadcast on television to an audience of more than half a billion people. They took the awestruck world on a tour of the Moon, describing craters, mountains, and future landing sites. They talked about the long shadows, cast by the rising and setting Sun, that made the moonscape look jagged and sinister.

But Earth itself made the greatest impression on both the astronauts and the watching world. Jim Lovell said that Earth was a "grand oasis in the big vastness of space."

Apollo 8 crossed once again into silence behind the Moon. The spacecraft could return home only if the rocket engine fired. If it failed, the astronauts would remain in lunar orbit forever.

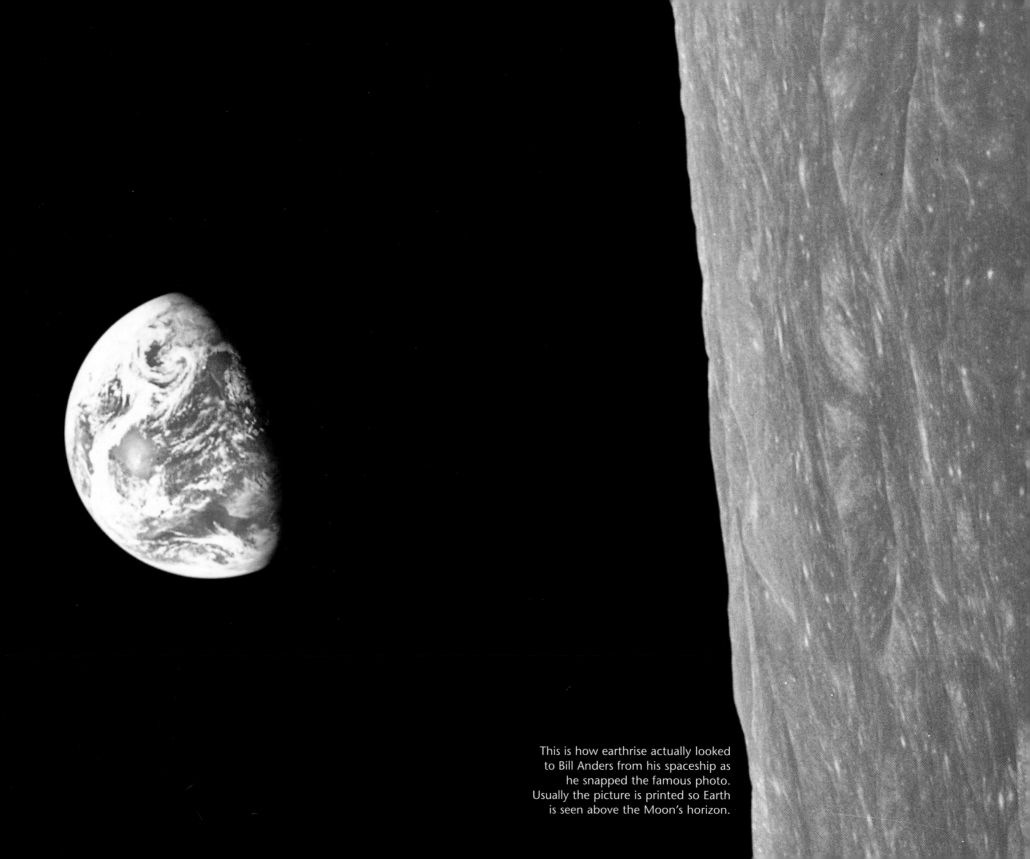

This is how earthrise actually looked
to Bill Anders from his spaceship as
he snapped the famous photo.
Usually the picture is printed so Earth
is seen above the Moon's horizon.

Scientists at Mission Control waited anxiously. Jim Lovell's voice broke the silence as the spaceship emerged from behind the moon.

"Please be informed," he exclaimed, "there is a Santa Claus!"

The engine had worked. On Christmas Day, *Apollo 8* headed for home—back to the little blue marble in space. The mission was a perfect success.

Apollo 8 had orbited the Moon ten times, photographing it and gathering information about its surface. In addition to these important scientific achievements, humans had seen an earthrise for the very first time.

The many craters on the farside are the result of billions of years of bombardment by meteors.

An *Apollo 8* flight director at his console in the Mission Control center.

Apollo 11 is launched from the Kennedy Space Center at 9:32 A.M. on July 16, 1969. Onboard are astronauts Neil A. Armstrong (commander), Michael Collins (command module pilot), and Edwin E. "Buzz" Aldrin Jr. (lunar module pilot).

Although the Soviets put the first man and woman into space and accomplished the first unmanned lunar landing, they ultimately lost the race to the Moon. On July 3, 1969, all hopes of a manned moon landing literally went up in smoke as the Soviet rocket exploded on the launchpad. For America, it was now simply a race against time.

It was July 20, 1969, 3:16 P.M. Houston time. Apollo 11's computer-controlled lunar module, called Eagle, was headed straight for a field of boulders on the Moon. With less than sixty seconds' worth of fuel left, Commander Neil Armstrong took the controls and steered Eagle toward safer ground.

Moondust swirled under the engine. Then, all was quiet. Armstrong's voice broke the silence.

"Houston, Tranquility Base here. The Eagle has landed!"

A brilliant rising sun cast long shadows across the bleak landscape. Beyond the horizon there was only the blackness of space.

Flight controllers at Mission Control in Houston, Texas, celebrate the lunar landing.

Sixty-nine miles above the lunar surface, *Apollo 11* astronaut Michael Collins circled the moon in the command module *Columbia*. Traveling at 3,700 miles per hour, he searched the Moon's surface for *Eagle*. Even with the help of a computerized sextant, an instrument used in navigation, Collins never spotted *Eagle* during his twenty-two hours alone in *Columbia*.

While flying above the Moon's near side, Collins could hear his crewmates even though he couldn't see them. He listened spellbound as Armstrong and Aldrin prepared to leave the lunar module for the first-ever moon walk.

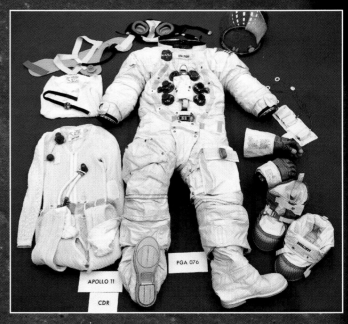

Neil Armstrong's space suit was fifteen layers thick and had five hundred parts. It carried oxygen, pumps, tubes, and cooling water to control the temperature inside the suit. It took Armstrong two hours to get dressed.

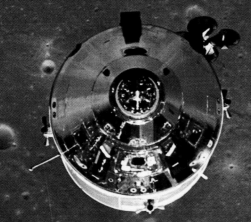

Columbia, as photographed from the lunar module.

Buzz Aldrin steps onto the Moon. "Magnificent desolation!" exclaimed Aldrin as he let go of the ladder.

As Buzz Aldrin opened the hatch and Neil Armstrong moved onto the ladder, *Columbia* flew behind the Moon's farside. Mike Collins couldn't hear Armstrong speak as he stepped onto the Moon, but millions of people back on Earth could:

"That's one small step for man, one giant leap for mankind."

Armstrong had planned to say, "That's one small step for *a* man, one giant leap for mankind," but he was so excited that he forgot to say the word *a* in the now-famous quote.

Armstrong took pictures and collected some powdery black soil before the amazed Aldrin joined him on the Moon's surface.

Buzz Aldrin, with Neil Armstrong reflected in his visor. The small, repeating plus signs burned into the film are camera-lens grid marks used for measuring distances on the Moon.

Six hundred million people watched and listened as Aldrin and Armstrong unfurled and raised an American flag on the Sea of Tranquility. The flag only looked like it was flying; wires stiffened the Stars and Stripes into a permanent flutter above the airless moonscape.

Throughout history, explorers have claimed newly discovered territory by flying their country's flag. But no one nation owns the Moon. It belongs to all people—past, present, and future. The astronauts did not claim the Moon for the United States. Instead, they celebrated their achievement with their fellow Americans and the world.

A remote-control camera shows the astronauts raising the flag. In 1967 the United Nations announced the Outer Space Treaty, which stated that "the Moon shall be the province of all mankind."

Buzz Aldrin faces the American flag and the rising Sun.

sent pictures back to Earth.

Now there was work to do. Aldrin and Armstrong
set up a seismometer to detect moonquakes, as
well as a laser reflector for measuring the distance
between the Moon and Earth to within centimeters.
They also collected twenty-two kilograms (about
forty-seven pounds) of rocks and soil. Since the
Moon's gravity is one sixth of Earth's, the
astronauts felt lighter and described the way
they walked on the Moon as
"kangaroo hopping."

Aldrin and Armstrong spent less than one Earth day—just twenty-one hours and thirty-six minutes—on the Moon's surface. Their moon walk lasted for only two hours and thirty-one minutes. Despite their rush, the astronauts felt as if they were on a world where time almost stood still. One lunar day lasts about a month: It takes twenty-nine and a half days for the Moon to make one full spin on its axis. On any one place on the Moon, the sun shines for two weeks followed by another two weeks of dark night.

There on the Sea of Tranquility, during the brief early hours of that lunar morning, our universe was forever expanded. Our dream of touching the ancient, mysterious Moon had finally come true.

Because there are no major forces of erosion on the Moon, an astronaut's footprint could remain there for millions of years.

A tired, but happy, Commander Neil Armstrong inside *Eagle* after the first moon walk.

Mike Collins's biggest fear about the entire *Apollo 11* mission was that he might have to return to Earth alone:

> As *Eagle*'s liftoff time approached, I got really nervous. If their engine didn't work, there was nothing I could do to rescue them from the surface. I simply had to come home by myself, leaving Neil and Buzz to die on the surface of the moon.
>
> —from *Flying to the Moon*, by Michael Collins. Farrar, Straus & Giroux, 1994.

The flag, photographed from inside the lunar module before liftoff. The astronauts had a hard time getting the flagpole to stand in the lunar soil, and during liftoff the flag was knocked over.

Michael Collins snapped this photograph of *Eagle*'s ascent, with Earth in the background. In that moment, Collins had captured all humanity on film except for himself.

The *Apollo 11* command module is hoisted out of the Pacific Ocean on July 24, 1969.

Fortunately, *Eagle* blasted off the Moon and was safely reunited with *Columbia*. Now the astronauts were on their way home to parades and parties. John F. Kennedy's goal had been achieved.

Apollo 11 fulfilled the dream of sending explorers to the Moon. It also answered important scientific questions. The seismometer proved that moonquakes are rare. Scientists learned from the rock samples that parts of the Moon were once hot with flowing volcanic lava. New minerals were also discovered. Armalcolite, a new type of titanium, was named after Armstrong, Aldrin, and Collins.

A ticker-tape parade for the *Apollo 11* astronauts.

From 1969 to 1972, six more Apollo spacecraft traveled to the Moon. Five missions actually got there. *Apollo 13* never landed because of an explosion in an oxygen tank.

Charles Conrad examines the TV camera on *Surveyor 3*, an unmanned probe that had landed on the Moon in 1967.

Apollo 12 lunar module pilot Alan Bean, with astronaut Charles Conrad Jr. reflected in his visor. The notebook on Bean's left wrist lists tasks to be completed.

Alan B. Shepard Jr., *Apollo 14*'s commander (and the first American in space ten years earlier in 1961), plants the third flag on the Moon in 1971. The second flag had been raised by the *Apollo 12* astronauts in 1969.

with each lunar landing, scientists discovered new information about the Moon. They learned that the Moon is ancient: about four and one-half billion years old.

The Apollo Moon rocks also suggested that the Moon was formed in a hot and violent crash after an early Mars-sized object collided with Earth. The Moon was formed from the dust and gas that flew into space after the crash.

Astronaut John Young kicks up moondust in the "grand prix" run of the lunar rover at the *Apollo 16* landing site. The rover's top speed was eleven miles per hour.

James Irwin scoops lunar soil during one of three moon walks. Long-duration backpacks allowed *Apollo 15* astronauts to spend extended periods of time exploring.

Apollo 16 was the first exploration of the Moon's central highlands. Here astronaut Charles M. Duke Jr. collects samples at the edge of a crater.

Apollo 16's commander, John W. Young, demonstrates the effect of one sixth of Earth's gravity by jumping three feet off the ground.

Apollo 17 astronaut Harrison "Jack" Schmitt was the first professional scientist to explore the Moon. Here he collects samples with a lunar rake.

Jack Schmitt discovered this orange soil, magnified here 160 times. The soil provided clues about the age, composition, and origin of the Moon.

The *Apollo 17* mission commander, Eugene A. Cernan, test-drives the lunar rover before loading it up with gear.

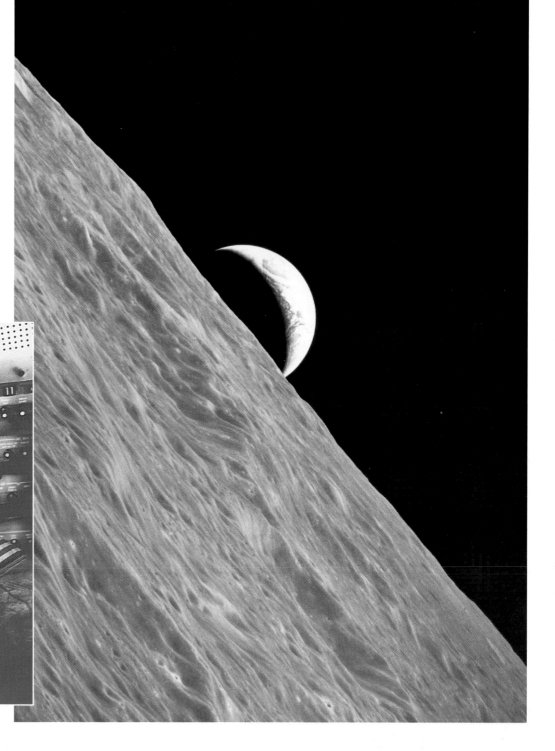

An *Apollo 17* photo of the rising crescent Earth above the lunar horizon.

Cernan, exhausted and filthy after his second of three moon walks. On December 13, 1972, he left the last footprints on the Moon.

After the *Apollo 17* mission, NASA focused on other projects, such as the space shuttle. In 1998 the United States returned to the Moon. For almost two years *Lunar Prospector,* an unmanned probe, orbited the Moon from sixty-three miles up. Information collected from *Prospector,* such as the size of the Moon's core and the amounts of gold, platinum, and iridium in moon rocks, supported the theory that the Moon was formed after an enormous object collided with Earth.

Prospector also discovered frozen water at the lunar poles and mapped the location of metals, such as aluminum and titanium, that might someday be mined for use on Earth. The probe also studied the Moon's magnetic fields and gravity.

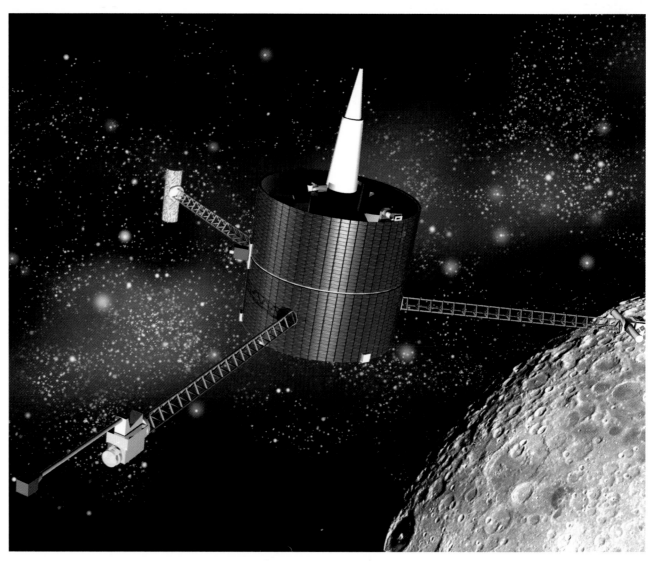

An artist's drawing of *Lunar Prospector* orbiting the Moon.

Today many astronauts and scientists think we should return to the Moon. Some astronomers believe that the Moon is the perfect place from which to study the universe. Moonquakes are a million times less likely than earthquakes, making the Moon a quiet, stable platform on which to build sensitive telescopes. The two weeks of nighttime on the Moon make it easier to study the stars, and with no atmosphere to blur the view, the stars are visible even in daylight.

An imagined lunar mining factory takes oxygen from rich volcanic soil.

This drawing of a futuristic Moon camp includes inflatable living spaces, radio antennae, a telescope, storage tanks, and all-terrain vehicles.

Sending people back to the Moon would be very costly. If cheaper rocket-launching systems can be developed, then more scientific Moon missions could occur. Private businesses might also send workers to the Moon to mine minerals or operate solar power stations. Even tourist flights to the Moon could be in our future.

Many scientists believe that humans will visit Mars during the first half of the twenty-first century.

Only twelve humans have walked on the Moon. Others may follow. Now we dream of exploring more of our solar system. A round-trip mission to Mars could take two years or more. The challenges are great, but our need to explore, to discover, and to succeed is even greater.

When astronauts raise the flag once again, we will all experience the adventure as we share in the ancient desire to understand our place in the universe.

This solar system montage (not to scale) was created using photographs taken by five separate spacecraft. From top to bottom are images of Mercury (by *Mariner 10*), Venus (by *Magellan*), Earth, the Moon (both by *Galileo*), Mars (by *Viking*), Jupiter, Saturn, Uranus, and Neptune (all by *Voyager*). The *Voyager* probes did not visit Pluto.

A view of Hadley Rille, a long, narrow valley on the Moon.

MOON EXPLORATION TIME LINE

ca. 2000 B.C.

Stonehenge is built to keep track of celestial events.

ca. 270 B.C.

Greek astronomer Aristarchus estimates the distance between Earth and the Moon as 60 Earth radii. The true distance varies between 55 and 63 Earth radii (354,000–404,000 km, or about 220,000–251,000 miles).

1610

Galileo Galilei publishes *The Starry Messenger*.

1647

Polish astronomer Johannes Hevelius draws maps of the Moon and names many of its features in his book *Selenographia*.

1750

German astronomer Johann Tobias Mayer discovers the Moon's libration zones, or the edges of the farside that occasionally wobble into view.

1840s

Some of the first photographs ever taken are of the Moon.

1865

Author Jules Verne writes the science fiction novel *From the Earth to the Moon*, in which three space travelers are launched out of a cannon.

1903

(December 17) The Wright brothers pilot the first airplane.

1920s

Robert Goddard and other space enthusiasts build and launch rockets.

1957

(October 4) The Soviet Union launches the first satellite, *Sputnik I*.

1958

(January 31) The United States launches its first satellite, *Explorer 1*.
(July 28) The National Aeronautics and Space Administration (NASA) is created.

1959

(October) The Soviet unmanned mission *Luna 1* takes photographs of the lunar farside.

1961

(April 12) Soviet cosmonaut Yuri Gagarin pilots *Vostok*, the world's first spacecraft, becoming the first human in space and the first to orbit Earth.

1962

(February 20) John Glenn is the first American to orbit Earth.

1963

(June 16) Soviet cosmonaut Valentina Tereshkova is the first woman in space.

1965

(March 18) Soviet cosmonaut Aleksei Leonov is history's first space walker.
(June 3) Edward White is the first American to walk in space.

1966

(January 31) The unmanned Soviet *Luna 9* makes the first soft landing on the Moon. It lands gently, instead of crashing into the lunar surface.
(March 31) *Luna 10* is the first lunar orbiter.
(May 30) The first American soft lander is *Surveyor 1*.

1967

(January 27) A fire in *Apollo 1* kills three American astronauts.
(November 9) The unmanned *Saturn V* rocket is launched for the first time.

1968

(October 11-22) *Apollo 7* is the first manned Apollo mission.
(December 21-27) *Apollo 8* is the first manned flight to orbit the moon.

1969

(March 3-13) *Apollo 9* tests the Apollo spacecraft while in Earth's orbit.
(May 18-26) *Apollo 10* brings the lunar module to within 9.4 miles (15 km) of the Moon's surface.
(July 20) *Apollo 11* makes the first lunar landing. A plaque left on the Moon reads: "Here men from the planet Earth first set foot upon the Moon, July 1969 A.D. We came in peace for all mankind."
(November 14-24) *Apollo 12* makes the first pinpoint lunar landing when the lunar module touches down about 600 feet from the unmanned U.S. lander *Surveyor 3*.

1970

(April 13) An explosion cripples the *Apollo 13* command module, forcing the astronauts to use their lunar module as a lifeboat for the journey home.
(September 12) The Soviet *Luna 16* is the first unmanned mission to return lunar soil samples to Earth.

1971

(January 31-February 9) *Apollo 14* is the first mission devoted to scientific exploration of the Moon.
(July 26-August 7) *Apollo 15* is another scientific expedition and the first to use the lunar rover.

1972

(April 16-27) *Apollo 16* is the first exploration of the lunar highlands.
(December 7-19) *Apollo 17* is the final mission and the longest Apollo flight.

1990

Japan sends *Muses A*, an unmanned orbiter, around the Moon.

1994

The U.S. sends the unmanned orbiter *Clementine* to map the Moon.

1998-1999

The American unmanned probe *Lunar Prospector* orbits the Moon to map it and conduct scientific research.

For my sons: Sasha, Rory, and Leo;
and for everyone else who loves rockets, space suits, and flags.

Recommended Web Sites

NASA Sites

NASA Home Page
http://www.nasa.gov/
(The first step for navigating NASA's vast Internet resource. Of special note are links to a site for kids and a multimedia gallery of NASA's complete image archives.)

Apollo Lunar Surface Journal
http://www.hq.nasa.gov/alsj/main.html
(History, scientific information, links, photographs, and much more.)

Exploring the Moon
http://cass.jsc.nasa.gov/moon.html
(Information on the various NASA Moon missions, hosted by the Lunar and Planetary Institute.)

StarChild: A Learning Center for Young Astronomers
http://starchild.gsfc.nasa.gov/docs/StarChild/StarChild.html
(Information provided about the solar system, the universe, and space travel, with links to many resources.)

Other Web Sites

Kids Earth and Sky
http://www.earthsky.com/Kids/
(Web site of a daily science radio series; features articles, views of tonight's sky, sections for teachers and kids, and many links.)

Welcome to Heavens-Above
http://www.heavens-above.com/
(Explore the night sky from any location on Earth.)

Moon Phases
http://www.googol.com/moon/
(See the phase of the Moon for every day of the month.)

spaceKids.com
http://www.spacekids.com/
(Information, activities, and contests.)

Recommended Books

Collins, Michael. *Flying to the Moon: An Astronaut's Story*. New York: Farrar Straus Giroux, 1994.

Fraser, Mary Ann. *One Giant Leap*. New York: Henry Holt and Company, 1993.

Gibbons, Gail. *The Moon Book*. New York: Holiday House, 1997.

Light, Michael. *Full Moon*. New York: Alfred A. Knopf, 1999.

Sis, Peter. *Starry Messenger*. New York: Farrar, Straus & Giroux, 1996.

Text copyright © 2001 by Alexandra Siy
All rights reserved, including the right of reproduction in whole or in part in any form.

Published by Charlesbridge Publishing
85 Main Street, Watertown, MA 02472
(617) 926-0329
www.charlesbridge.com

Library of Congress Cataloging-in-Publication Data
Siy, Alexandra.
Footprints on the moon/Alexandra Siy.
p.   cm.
Includes bibliographical references.
ISBN 1-57091-408-7 (reinforced for library use)
ISBN 1-57091-409-5 (softcover)
1. Project Apollo (U.S.)—History—Juvenile literature. 2. Space flight to the moon—History—Juvenile literature. 3. Space race—Juvenile literature. [1. Project Apollo (U.S.) 2. Space flight to the moon. 3. Space race.] I. Title.
TL789.8.U6 A5818   2001
629.45'4'0973—dc21   00-038370

Printed in the United States of America
(hc) 10 9 8 7 6 5 4 3 2 1
(sc) 10 9 8 7 6 5 4 3 2 1

Display type and text type set in Horizon, Garamond, and Stone Sans
Color separations by Eastern Rainbow, Derry, New Hampshire
Printed and bound by Phoenix Color, Rockaway, New Jersey
Production supervision by Brian G. Walker
Designed by Diane M. Earley

Acknowledgments

I extend special thanks to the *Apollo 16* commander, Captain John Young, for sharing his experiences and insights with me about Apollo, the Moon, and the future of space exploration. I am also indebted to my talented editors, Yolanda LeRoy and Harold Underdown, for their enthusiasm and wisdom; to book designer Diane Earley for her terrific work; and to R. Bruce Ward of the Harvard-Smithsonian Center for Astrophysics and Wally Schirra, the *Apollo 7* commander, for their expert readings.

I am grateful to the many people at NASA who helped me obtain photographs, especially Sherie Jefferson at the NASA Lyndon B. Johnson Space Center and Lisa Chu Thielbar at the NASA Ames Research Center. Thanks also to Roger Arno of the NASA Ames Research Center for his futuristic space art. For their photographic research assistance, thanks to James B. Hill of the John Fitzgerald Kennedy Library; Cathy Houghton at the English Heritage Photographic Library; Franca Principe of Istituto e Museo di Storia della Scienza; Robin Witmore at the UCO/Lick Observatory; and John Cunningham of Visuals Unlimited.

To my husband, Eric, thank you for your excellent critique and your extraordinary patience. To our daughter, Melissa, thanks for babysitting while I was far off in another world.

Photograph Credits

p. 2: © C. P. George, Visuals Unlimited; p. 3: (all images) UCO/Lick Observatory; p. 4: (bottom left) © English Heritage Photographic Library; p. 5: (top left) Library of Congress LC-USZ62-95171, (right) Library of Congress LC-USZ62-122699, (bottom left) Istituto e Museo di Storia della Scienza; p. 6: (background) Library of Congress LC-USZ62-6166-A; p. 7: (bottom left) Photo #ST-A13-60-62 in the John F. Kennedy Library; p. 26: NASA Ames Research Center/Roger Arno; p. 27: (right) NASA Ames Research Center/Roger Arno; p. 28: NASA Ames Research Center/Pat Rawlings; p. 29: photoNASA/jpl/caltech; all other photos are from NASA.

APOLLO 11

APOLLO XII

Conrad • Gordon • Bean

APOLLO XIII

EX LUNA, SCIENTIA

APOLLO XVII

CERNAN • EVANS • SCHMITT

APOLLO 11

APO

Conra

APOLLO 15

SCOTT WORDEN IRWIN

APOLLO 16

YOUNG • MATTINGLY • DUKE

APOLLO XVII

CERNAN • EVANS • SCHMITT